GOOD·OLD·DAYS

Live It Again™

1948

JOHN FALTER

Dear Friends,

On the mend and on the move—that would describe not only the United States as 1948 dawned, but also most of the world. The pain and deprivation of World War II was fresh enough in our memories, but inexorably we were moving forward.

Perhaps the best marker of that progress was the 1948 Winter Olympics held in St. Moritz, Switzerland in late January. For the first time in a dozen years the Olympics were free from the horrors of war. Of course, the selection of a neutral country was a nod to the frayed nerves of a war-weary world, and neither Germany nor Japan was invited to the Games, but the event was good international therapy. By the time the Summer Olympics were held in London in June, the field had grown from 28 to 59 countries represented.

A growing economy fueled our appetite to travel.

A growing economy fueled our appetite to travel. No longer shackled by frozen automobile production and the rationing of gasoline and tires, vacationing baby-booming families invaded resorts, beaches and national parks. Many were even enticed to move lock, stock and barrel to the new frontier of American life: the suburbs.

Live it all again as the photographs and stories in this wonderful book take you back to 1948—the days when we were on the mend and on the move.

Contents

FUTURAMIC

© 1948 SEPS

REPRINTED WITH PERMISSION FROM WHIRLPOOL CORPORATION

REPRINTED WITH PERMISSION FROM HART, SCHAFFNER & MARX

NARA, TRUMAN LIBRARY

Neighborhood commerce, such as delivery of dry cleaning to the doorstep, was indicative of an economy on the rise following the end of World War II.

Everyday Life

Around the neighborhood

By 1948, it had been a few years since soldiers returned from World War II and restrictions on gasoline, various foods and household items were lifted. Americans were settling into a stronger economy and sense of stability, which brought new spirit to everyday living. With the cost of gasoline averaging 16 cents a gallon, friends and family members were willing to travel again to see each other and enjoy reunions.

Families continued to enjoy pre-war activities, such as playing a neighborhood game of baseball or enjoying a bicycle ride, but they also gradually adopted a new type of family entertainment with the popularity of radio and the rise of television.

A day of fishing, a pastime that was still popular, was even a favorite of the family pet.

Neighbors and families gathered outside to enjoy working together in their yards.

The Metro Daily News

FINAL EDITION

JANUARY 5, 1948

WARNER BROTHERS SHOWS FIRST COLOR NEWSREEL

Everyday Life
Kids' life

Mothers spent special moments reading books to children, a bonding time for all.

Both Mom and Dad spent quality time with children by attending such special events as plays, musicals and children's programs. In most families, nothing was more important than supporting events and accomplishments of family members.

"I came down to tell you there's an octopus under the tub. Can I have some cake?"

Evening was a time to bond as a family after a long hard day. Kids spent time playing board games or working on homework with parents. The quality of such times together created an appreciation for family heritage and teamwork that lasted for a lifetime.

SALE
EARMUFFS
98¢

"Got the same color in a smaller size?"

The Metro Daily News
FINAL EDITION

JANUARY 30, 1948

ORVILLE WRIGHT, AVIATION PIONEER, DIES

Winter Olympics

St. Moritz, Switzerland

The 1948 Winter Olympics was held in St. Moritz, Switzerland, and was the first Olympics since 1936, due to World War II. Although the winter event was held in a neutral country, the exclusion of Japan and Germany created a tense atmosphere in spite of the fact that the war had ended. Regardless, these Olympics marked a return to international cooperation.

Organizing the event was difficult due to the lack of resources after the war. But these difficulties were overcome and the opening ceremonies, shown at right, took place on January 30. By the close of the Games, 670 athletes from 28 nations competed in 22 events.

Blue = Participating for the first time

Green = Have previously participated

Yellow square = host city St. Moritz, Switzerland

MAP REPRINTED WITH PERMISSION OF CREATOR FIREFOX13

Figure skater Dick Button lands a jump as the audience watches his performance during the men's figure skating competition. Button impressed the judges at St. Moritz, as well as the crowds, winning the gold medal. He is credited for having been the first skater to land the double axel jump in 1948, as well as being the youngest man, at age 18, to win an Olympic gold in figure skating.

American skier Gretchen Fraser smiles as she poses for a portrait after winning the slalom race. Fraser had the dual honor of winning the first American gold medal for skiing and of being the first American gold medalist overall in these Olympics. She made America proud once again when she later won the silver medal for the alpine combined race.

Joseph Meconi sits grinning and ready to drive the American four-man bobsleigh team to victory and a gold medal. The victory wasn't without some extra drama, though, as questions arose about a possible sabotaging of the American bobsleighs. The mystery was solved after a truck driver admitted to accidentally hitting the shed where the bobsleds were housed, and the U.S. team was able to repair the damaged equipment before its races.

Although the USA hockey team did not win any medals, they displayed admirable sportsmanship and true Olympic spirit by exchanging handshakes and hockey sweaters with the Swiss team before a game.

Winter Escape

© 1948 SEPS

"I can't see it! First of all it breaks up your whole winter ..."

This year, let TWA take you to

The lands where winter is fun

A playful snowball fight after a day of skiing was a fun way to end a winter vacation day. Many airlines, like TWA, offered to take travelers away to "lands where winter is fun," and visitors enjoyed all that the snow brought to a mountain town.

Skiing was a popular winter activity, both in the United States and Europe. The Winter Olympics showed off the skills of many skiers, inspiring others to take up the sport.

Americans were encouraged to travel to far-off countries like Switzerland where they could learn about the Swiss culture as well as enjoy the breathtaking scenes of a country that really showed its beauty in the winter.

Many Americans could only dream about an escape from the drudgery of winter. While these two work in the cold and snow, they are tantalized with the thought of a beach vacation getaway.

The Metro Daily News

FINAL EDITION

THE WEATHER
City and State—Rain,
Snow, Colder
(Details in Daily Almanac)

THE ASSOCIATED PRESS
THE UNITED PRESS

VOLUME 97 — No. 161   20 PAGES   FIVE CENTS

JANUARY 30, 1948

MAHATMA GANDHI ASSASSINATED

The respected political and spiritual leader known for his belief in nonviolent resistance is shot by extreme nationalist Nathuram Godse.

Travel the World

The world of air travel became much larger following World War II. Airlines advertised to inspire Americans to travel the world to far-off countries in Europe, Asia and even Australia. The world seemed to be open for Americans as air travel became more prevalent and affordable. Airlines encouraged America's dreams of travel and showed the far-away and exotic as accessible.

FAMOUS BIRTHDAYS

Rick James, February 1 Motown singer

Alice Cooper, February 4 Rock singer

Bernadette Peters, February 28 Actress

Is INDIA
really far away?
(only 2½ days by TWA)

REPRINTED WITH PERMISSION FROM AMERICAN AIRLINES, INC.

So smooth... so fast...
this new road
to ROME

© PAN AMERICAN WORLD AIRWAYS,
INC., USED WITH PERMISSION

Across the Pacific

© PAN AMERICAN WORLD AIRWAYS, INC., USED WITH PERMISSION

Now, see those
castles in SPAIN

REPRINTED WITH PERMISSION FROM AMERICAN AIRLINES, INC.

At the Movies

Laurence Olivier, shown here with his wife, actress Vivian Leigh, tackled *Hamlet* on the big screen and was rewarded with an Oscar for Best Actor. The film also nabbed the Academy Award for Best Picture.

1948 brought an era of drama and mystery to the theaters. Moviegoers were ready to face more serious stories after a break from the light-hearted musicals which often dominated motion pictures in the 1940s.

Westerns like *Red River* were as popular as ever during that decade, but the more sinister mysteries of Alfred Hitchcock and John Huston also caught the attention of American movie fans. But not all was dark and dreary on the silver screen in 1948. Irving Berlin cheered up audiences with the highly popular and star-studded *Easter Parade*.

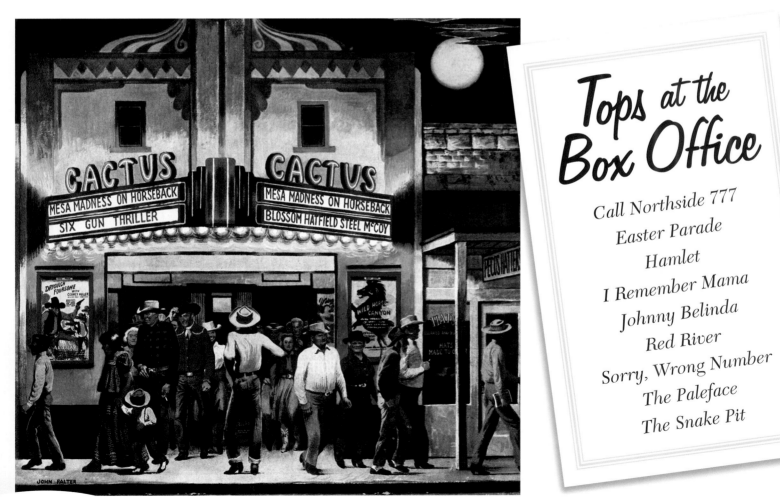

Tops at the Box Office

Call Northside 777
Easter Parade
Hamlet
I Remember Mama
Johnny Belinda
Red River
Sorry, Wrong Number
The Paleface
The Snake Pit

THE HAPPIEST MUSICAL EVER MADE IS

IRVING **BERLIN'S**

EASTER PARADE

M·G·M

Color by **TECHNICOLOR**

Songs
EASTER PARADE
HAPPY EASTER
DRUM CRAZY
IT ONLY HAPPENS
WHEN I DANCE WITH YOU
MICHIGAN
A FELLA WITH AN UMBRELLA
SHAKIN' THE BLUES AWAY
STEPPIN' OUT WITH MY BABY
COUPLE OF SWELLS
MAGAZINE COVER
BETTER LUCK NEXT TIME
EVERYBODY'S DOING IT
BEAUTIFUL FACES
I LOVE A PIANO
SNOOKY OOKUMS
RAGTIME VIOLIN
ALABAMA CHOO CHOO
and many others

starring

JUDY **GARLAND** · FRED **ASTAIRE**

PETER **LAWFORD** · ANN **MILLER** · *Screen Play by* Sidney Sheldon, Frances Goodrich and Albert Hackett
Original Story by Frances Goodrich and Albert Hackett
A Metro-Goldwyn-Mayer Picture

Lyrics by **IRVING BERLIN** · *Musical Numbers* **ROBERT ALTON** · *Directed by* **CHARLES WALTERS** · *Produced by* **ARTHUR FREED**

COPYRIGHT BY METRO-GOLDWYN-MAYER INC. ALL RIGHTS RESERVED

THE WEATHER
City and State—Fair,
Warm, Colder
Later in forty tomorrow

The Metro Daily News

VOLUME 57—No. 103

FINAL
EDITION

20 PAGES · FIVE CENTS

MARCH 8, 1948

SUPREME COURT RULES SEPARATION BETWEEN CHURCH AND STATE

Says no to religious instruction in public schools.

Judy Garland and Fred Astaire paired up to play Broadway performers in *Easter Parade*—roles which were not too far from their own careers as actors who often performed in musicals. Irving Berlin won an Academy Award for his scoring of the film, as well as gave moviegoers memorable songs such as "Steppin' Out With My Baby."

At the Movies

NOTHING EVER HELD YOU LIKE ALFRED HITCHCOCK'S

ROPE

STARRING

JAMES STEWART

IN COLOR BY TECHNICOLOR

Presented by WARNER BROS.

JOHN DALL · FARLEY GRANGER · SIR CEDRIC HARDWICKE

CONSTANCE COLLIER · JOAN CHANDLER

A TRANSATLANTIC PICTURES PRODUCTION

Although *Joan of Arc* was not initially popular at the box office or considered very significant, actress Ingrid Bergman was nominated for a Best Actress Oscar for her starring role in the film. Bergman had played the role earlier in a successful Broadway play, *Joan of Lorraine*, and had petitioned for many years to make a film of the play.

Rope, directed by Alfred Hitchcock and adapted from a play by Patrick Hamilton, placed Jimmy Stewart's character in the middle of an ominous party where a missing guest, unbeknownst to his family and fiancé, has actually been murdered by two of his former classmates. The style of the film is notable for playing out its psychological drama in "real time," which adds tension to the movie.

Humphrey Bogart appeared in two popular John Huston films in 1948. He played a gold prospector in Mexico whose greed leads to his demise in *The Treasure of the Sierra Madre*, and he also played opposite his wife, Lauren Bacall, in the crime drama *Key Largo*.

Tops at the Box Office

Abbott and Costello Meet Frankenstein

Fort Apache

Joan of Arc

Key Largo

Rope

State of the Union

The Red Shoes

The Three Musketeers

The Treasure of the Sierra Madre

Moira Shearer displayed her dancing skills playing a young ballerina in the film *The Red Shoes*. The film, which is based on a Hans Christian Anderson story, follows a ballerina's rise to fame and her quest for love. It is often named a favorite by filmmakers, including Martin Scorsese.

THE WEATHER
City and Snow—Rain,
Snow, Colder

The Metro Daily News

FINAL EDITION

26 PAGES   FIVE CENTS

VOLUME 87 — No. 281

MARCH 17, 1948

HELLS ANGELS MOTORCYCLE GANG IS FOUNDED IN CALIFORNIA

Music and Radio

With all of the innovations in home entertainment, the radio and phonograph became important in family entertainment. Whether gathering to listen to a voice croon a beloved tune or a narrator continue to unfold the ongoing saga of a favorite character, family members often spent a few evening hours together in front of the radio.

Records were also popular, especially with the new 33⅓ long playing size that Columbia Records developed. While some people were still playing the big band and swing music that dominated the earlier part of the decade, top hits for 1948 showed that a new era of solo singers, like Dinah Shore, Nat King Cole and Doris Day, had begun.

© GETTY IMAGES

Dinah Shore had tried for many years to secure a place as a singer for a swing orchestra, but was not successful. Her loss became a gain when she started her career as a solo singer. In 1948, she soared to the top of the charts with the song "Buttons and Bows." Her popularity continued through the next decade with many more radio hits and movie roles.

Top Hits of 1948

"Buttons and Bows" Dinah Shore

"Nature Boy" Nat King Cole

"I'm Looking Over a Four Leaf Clover" Art Mooney

"Twelfth Street Rag" Pee Wee Hunt

"Bumble Boogie" Freddy Martin

"A Tree In The Meadow" Margaret Whiting

"I've Got My Love To Keep Me Warm" Les Brown

"It's Magic" Doris Day

"Mañana (Is Soon Enough For Me)" Peggy Lee

"Woody Woodpecker" Kay Kyser

"You Call Everybody Darlin" Al Trace

"You Can't Be True, Dear" Ken Griffin

The Metro Daily News

THE WEATHER
City still Damn Rain.
Snow. Colder
details in day journal

FINAL EDITION

10 PAGES   FIVE CENTS

VOLUME 97—No. 161

MARCH 22, 1948

VOICE OF FIRESTONE BROADCASTS WIDELY

It is the first radio program to air on both AM and FM radio stations.

Musicals were also family favorites for at-home listening. Here, Oscar Hammerstein, Irving Berlin and Richard Rodgers form a musical powerhouse as they listen to auditions for an upcoming play. Berlin had a bright year in 1948 because of the popularity of the songs he wrote for the film *Easter Parade*. Rodgers and Hammerstein also had a banner year; they were guests on the debut of the *Ed Sullivan Show* in June.

Radio Stars & Hits of 1948

The Adventures of Sam Spade

Duffy's Tavern

The Falcon

Fred Allen

The Green Hornet

Inner Sanctum

Jack Benny

The Lone Ranger

Suspense

This is Your FBI

Walter Winchell

Nat King Cole lit up the airwaves with his song "Nature Boy." While he started his career as a jazz pianist, Cole took to his signature tunes in the 1940s and became more recognized as a pop music singer. Here, Cole uses both his skills as a musician and singer to entertain guests at a party celebrating his impending wedding to Maria Ellington.

Suits, ties and dresses were still the order of the day when visiting friends and neighbors for a casual game of cards.

Norman Rockwell

© 1948 THE NORMAN ROCKWELL FAMILY ENTITIES

FAMOUS BIRTHDAYS
Steven Tyler, March 26 Singer, member of band Aerosmith
Al Gore, March 31 Environmentalist and former Vice President

"Never mind, dear. Here's one with fifty-two."

The game of croquet became an outdoor favorite at family reunions and get-togethers. It was often considered "exercise" following a hefty meal of home-cooked food.

© 1948 SEPS

"Who led that piece of salami?!!"

Casual wear and shorts began to work their way on to the scene as popular apparel for a nation enjoying times of fun and games once again.

Everyday Life
Home sweet home

Homes were built following plat maps, as farmlands around metropolitan areas began to turn into suburbs. The new arrangement created a whole new culture of community life, which included neighborhood cookouts, backyard fences and children playing with other children on the block. The concept of every house having a unique plan gave way to subdivisions where many of the homes looked almost exactly alike.

Wall-to-wall carpet, as opposed to hardwood floors, became more popular because it added warmth and safety to a home where families gathered to enjoy an evening together after a hard day of work.

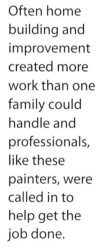

Often home building and improvement created more work than one family could handle and professionals, like these painters, were called in to help get the job done.

The Metro Daily News

THE WEATHER
City and State—Fair.
Snow, Colder.
Details in Daily Statement.

FINAL
EDITION

VOLUME 97 — No. 161

19 PAGES

FIVE CENTS

APRIL 7, 1948

WORLD HEALTH ORGANIZATION ESTABLISHED

United Nations founds specialized agency as an authority on international public health.

Post War Anecdotes

For a period of time after the end of WWII, *The Saturday Evening Post* encouraged servicemen to share stories of the lighter side of their experiences in the military. They called these stories "Post War Anecdotes." Here are a few of our favorites from 1948.

Tell Us What You Need, Joe

A   P O S T   W A R   A N E C D O T E

DURING the war, the brain boys in Washington were full of fine ideas for improving the efficiency of the military. One notion, tested in our Southern training camp, was to turn a group of soldiers loose in the mountains to find out what equipment the G. I. thought was most essential to his welfare. The soldiers were given all the materials they could use—tents, lumber, cooking equipment, tools, and so on—and left alone; the theory being that they would first build whatever structure they considered most important.

Soon after this group had been sent out, a party of official observers came to see what had hap-pened. Arrived at the camp site, the observers found no tents or buildings; but back in the woods they heard sounds of activity and soon they saw a large tent, carefully set up in a neatly cleared space and guarded by a sentry. Here, they told one another, would be the soldier's first essential need. Was it a chapel, they asked the guard. A mess hall? A sleeping tent?

The guard shook his head, lifted the entrance flap. Inside, clearly demonstrating careful and ingenious workmanship, were four fine craps tables, complete with banking boards and tacked-down blankets.

—STANLEY J. MEYER.

When Ignorance Was Bliss

A   P O S T   W A R   A N E C D O T E

WHILE I was flying from Italy to Africa with a group of naval officers in 1944, one motor of our twin-engine plane began to sputter threateningly. Immediately all the passengers but one, an elderly and salty-looking commodore, got greatly excited. This commodore didn't even glance up from the dispatches he was reading when the plane engine started to make odd noises; and he only looked up briefly when we nervously pointed to pieces of the left motor that were hurtling down to the Mediterranean Sea.

The pilot finally sent back word that we probably would be able to land safely, but we were still jittery when we came down at Bizerte for repairs. "There's nothing like long naval training," we told each other, sliding respectful glances toward the unruffled commodore. "Why, he didn't even bat an eye!"

As ranking officer, the commodore got off last, started to walk away—then turned abruptly to stare at the plane.

"Good Lord!" he said. "I thought it was amphibious!"

—T. A. REYNOLDS, JR.

By Their Fruits Ye Shall Know Them

ABOUT a year before Japan's surrender, the Office of Strategic Services sent a small group of American soldiers to the Japanese-held city of Bangkok in Thailand to get information on enemy activities. The mission was so super hush-hush that even in Washington only a few men knew of its existence. Elaborate codes and intricate signals had been arranged; the disguises of the soldiers were perfectly complete. They lived in a lonely shuttered house, creeping out to do their careful work only at night under the ever-watchful protection of the Thai underground.

After some months of very useful activity, the members of this mission began to congratulate themselves on their success. They doubted if even their nearest neighbors knew they were there, doing such an efficient job in this enemy city under constant threat of death.

Then their houseboy, a trusted underground agent, came trotting back from market where he had been buying some fruit. "Shopkeeper smile today," he reported. "He say Americans eat many, many bananas, don't they?"

—ADDISON R. BRAGG.

No Chance for Advancement

ONE night during the bitter fighting in the Cassino sector of the Italian front, my unit relieved a battalion that had been in the line for two weeks, with the enemy on Monte Cassino looking down their throats every minute of the time. Their slightest movement invited fire, and casualties had been very heavy.

As my platoon wriggled carefully up through the debris, I saw a mud-encrusted G. I. in a slit trench, his machine gun covering the doorway of a wineshop fifty yards away. Edging nearer, I said, "How• are things here, pretty hot?"

"Listen, Joe," he said wearily, "I was on Hill Six-oh-nine in Tunisia and I thought things were hot. I crossed the Volturno twice, and I thought things were hotter. But, brother, in this area, when they say, 'Advance,' I just lean forward in this here hole!"

—CHARLES F. STEWART.

Greetings From the Flagship

WITH all her lights extinguished, the U.S.S. Boise, in company with other cruisers and their destroyer screen, was steaming toward an Italian shore to carry out ·a surprise bombardment. Luckily, the night was utterly black, for enemy submarines were known to be in the vicinity.

Suddenly, to the horror of those on the bridge, the Boise burst into full illumination—her truck lights, running lights and battle identification lights all ablaze. Someone had accidentally tripped ·the master switch, for an awful moment making the Boise a glaring target outlined in red, white and green.

Swearing softly to himself, the captain awaited the inevitable reprimand from the flagship. It came, with exquisite sarcasm: "Merry Christmas!"

—J. W. JOHNSON.
Lt. Comdr., USNR.

The Marshall Plan

Rebuilding Europe

After World War II, Europe was devastated, economically and physically, with its cities in ruins and many people starving, raising fears that Western Europe, in its vulnerable state, would fall to Soviet control. Secretary of State George Marshall proposed that the United States help Europe with its rebuilding. President Truman responded by signing the Economic Recovery Act of 1948, which became known as the Marshall Plan. The United States' funding eventually reached over $12 billion, which helped spark European industrialization and, in turn, provided relief in the form of jobs, food and shelter to many Europeans.

The Marshall Plan still benefited Germany with economic aid, although just years before its creation U.S. soldiers were battling enemy German troops. This photograph of a worker rebuilding from the ashes of West Berlin shows the prominently displayed symbols of Berlin and the Marshall Plan side by side.

FOR EUROPEAN RECOVERY
SUPPLIED BY THE
UNITED STATES OF AMERICA

Secretary of State Marshall, pictured here discussing his plan with President Truman, Paul Hoffman and Averell Harriman, became the only general to be recognized for his humanitarian efforts with a Nobel Peace Prize.

Because of the partition, war and Israel's declaration of independence, most Arab families, like the citizens of Yehud, left their homes to move out of Israeli territory. Yehud was primarily an Arab city before 1948, when the entire Arab population left the newly-deemed Israeli city.

Dr. Chaim Weizmann, shown here presenting President Truman with a Torah, became the first President of Israel. Weizmann worked with President Truman to get United States' support for the new country. The United States officially recognized the State of Israel only 11 minutes after Israel declared its independence.

Israel Is Born

A new nation

In 1947, after many years of internal strife, Palestine was partitioned by the United Nations into a Jewish state, an Arab state and the UN-administered Jerusalem. Zionist leaders, who had been struggling for many years to gain a Jewish homeland in Palestine, accepted the division. However, most of the Arab population did not accept the UN proposal, which sparked an escalation that developed into a civil war. On May 14, 1948, Israel declared independence, technically ending the civil war, but not the conflicts between many Arab and Israeli groups.

Jewish crowds gathered outside Dizengoff House (now Independence Hall) with anticipation on May 14, waiting to hear Israel's Declaration of Independence.

"Don't shut me out behind your Iron Curtain, Baby …"

Allies unload milk as part of food-supply deliveries to Germans during the Berlin Blockade. Every day, more than 13,000 tons of food were delivered by Allied Forces during the airlift as anxious Berliners welcomed planes flying supplies to their city.

Sixtieth Troop Carrier Group C-54 Skymasters stand ready to bring supplies to West Berlin.

"Well, if there is another war, we ought to fight it by ourselves so we don't have any allies to argue with afterwards!"

The Berlin Blockade

The U.S. responds

The Berlin Blockade was the first international crisis of the Cold War. The Soviet Union, under Joseph Stalin, was beginning its push of communism into Europe. Stalin's immediate goal was to start supplying a recovering Berlin with food and fuel, with the aim of gaining Soviet control over the city.

The United States and other Western Allies, in contrast, wanted to keep Germany from Soviet control while still helping to rebuild the country.

When the Soviet Union blocked the Western Allies' railroad and road access to the parts of Berlin under their control, the Allies organized the Berlin Airlift to transport supplies to the people of West Berlin.

By April of 1949, it was clear that the efforts of the United States and other Western Allies were succeeding, to the dismay of the Soviets, and the blockade was lifted in May.

Skytrains lined up daily to unload supplies for Berlin residents. Western Allies completed hundreds of thousands of flights during the span of the Blockade.

What Made Us Laugh

"Maybe we'd better put a nickel in it anyway."

"I've seen as much as a half an hour go by
and none of them make a move."

"Oh, *brother!* He's going to file the points."

"Remember about the cod-liver oil for the children—call the diaper
service—my blue coat in the hall closet to the cleaners ..."

"Boy—it's going to be tough getting back into the old grind again."

"I know I promised you a new hat if I was elected—
but you know how I am about campaign promises"

"It's much more enjoyable if you sit back and close your eyes."

"And now we bring you another stirring chapter
in the life of Young Widder Green …"

President Truman tips his hat in greeting as he rides with African-American Governor William H. Hastie. Hastie went on in his career to become the first African-American Federal appeals court judge.

Copy of Executive Order 9981.

Integration and Opportunity

The road to equality

The sound of the whistle of the American Freedom Train could be heard throughout the land in 1948, chiming in with political voices crying for equal treatment of all individuals.

The train was a sign of times to come, with a growing cry for change when it came to restrictions and a lack of opportunity for minorities. Issues such as segregation and the lack of female enrollment in schools and universities became more contested.

At the Democratic Convention in 1948, voices from outspoken politicians such as Hubert Humphrey called for leaders to move from states' rights to human rights.

On July 26, President Truman made a strong stance by issuing Executive Order 9981, which called for desegregation in the Armed Services and equal treatment for all enlisted people.

EXECUTIVE ORDER

ESTABLISHING THE PRESIDENT'S COMMITTEE ON EQUALITY OF TREATMENT AND OPPORTUNITY IN THE ARMED SERVICES

WHEREAS it is essential that there be maintained in the armed services of the United States the highest standards of democracy, with equality of treatment and opportunity for all those who serve in our country's defense:

NOW, THEREFORE, by virtue of the authority vested in me as President of the United States, by the Constitution and the statutes of the United States, and as Commander in Chief of the armed services, it is hereby ordered as follows:

1. It is hereby declared to be the policy of the President that there shall be equality of treatment and opportunity for all persons in the armed services without regard to race, color, ...al origin. This policy shall be put into effect ...le, having due regard to the time required ...anges without impairing efficiency

Members of the Susan B. Anthony Club, an organization that had its roots in advocacy for women's suffrage, pose in front of the Freedom Train. The train, which carried copies of important historical documents, toured the country to remind Americans of the far-reaching liberty available to them in the United States.

young Hubert Humphrey delivered
fiery speech at the 1948 Democratic
onvention, advocating human rights
part of the party's political platform.

THE WEATHER
City and State—Fair,
Snow, Colder

The Metro Daily News

FINAL
EDITION

VOLUME 87 — No. 161

19 PAGES   FIVE CENTS

MAY 10, 1948

U.S. ARMY TAKES CONTROL OF THE RAILS

President Truman orders the Army to operate the railroads to prevent a threatened nationwide strike. The Army retains control until 1952.

Integration and Opportunity
In education

Although most public schools were segregated, like the all-African-American school shown above, there were some attempts in 1948 to move towards integration in education, laying the groundwork for the momentous Brown vs. Board of Education decision for desegregation in 1954.

Ada Lois Sipuel Fisher, seen here with Dr. J.E. Fellows, Amos T. Hall and Thurgood Marshall, sought enrollment in the graduate law program at the University of Oklahoma. Although initially denied her request, Sipuel Fisher filed suit against the Board of Regents and was admitted to the university in 1949.

FAMOUS BIRTHDAYS
Steve Winwood, May 12 Singer and musician
Stevie Nicks, May 26 Singer and member of band Fleetwood Mac
John Bonham, May 31 Drummer of band Led Zeppelin

Shirley Mae Dyson illustrates on a blackboard the ratio of men to women attending Glendale College in California, pointing out the need for more programs to attract female students to the college. In general, men far outweighed women in college attendance in 1948.

George McLaurin, a retired professor who already had a master's degree, applied to the all-white University of Oklahoma and was rejected because of state segregation laws. However, he won an appeal and was allowed to attend, but wasn't able to sit with his fellow students.

The opportunity to purchase gasoline without restriction made it possible to cruise, visit more distant places and expand opportunities for dating and fun with friends and family. Stylish automobiles began to sell as their combination of attraction and function was perfect for a night out.

Everyday Life

On the town

With the economy growing stronger and the worries of war farther behind, the sounds of jubilance and happiness could be heard echoing in the streets again.

Family and friend get-togethers became more prevalent and social life became more affordable. It was a nation bouncing back from the stresses of war.

Drive-in restaurants sprung up to serve customers cruising in their new cars. Record players reverberated big band music at local dances. Couples once again enjoyed dinner at a favorite restaurant. And, those owning the new novelty, black and white television, often invited friends and neighbors to share their favorite broadcasts.

FAMOUS BIRTHDAYS
Jerry Mathers, June 2 Actor in *Leave It to Beaver*
Dave Concepción, June 17 Baseball player
Kathy Bates, June 28 Actress

The Metro Daily News FINAL EDITION
JUNE 21, 1948
COLUMBIA RECORDS UNVEILS 33⅓ LP RECORD
It is the first long-playing microgroove record.

Summer Olympics

London, England

© GETTY IMAGES

After a 12-year absence due to World War II, the Summer Olympics were revived, with London playing host to the games. For the first time, the games were televised, allowing Americans to view the athletes from the United States and 58 other nations compete in the games. Germany and Japan, however, were barred from participating.

The Olympics included 33 track and field events and many team and individual sports, such as basketball, boxing, swimming, gymnastics and football. The United States closed the games with 84 medals, 38 of which were gold, making America by far the top medal-winning nation.

London, England

Blue = Participating for the first time

Green = Have previously participated

Yellow square = host city London

MAP REPRINTED WITH PERMISSION OF CREATOR FIREFOX13

On July 29, 1948, guardsmen marched around the track inside Wembly Stadium during the opening cermony of the London Olympics.

The official poster for 1948 games combined the ancient athletes of the early Olympics with modern London, showing a continuity with past Games and the tradition of the long-running competition.

Summer Olympics
Athletes in action

Zoe Ann Olsen gracefully sails through the air as she practices her diving before competing in the Games. Olsen, Patty Elsener and Vicki Draves made up the American springboard diving team. Together they won all three springboard diving medals, which they display proudly at right. While Olsen took the silver medal and Elsener took bronze, Draves surpassed expectations by winning gold medals in both springboard and platform diving.

American Harrison Dillard had to give one last push to edge out fellow American Barney Ewell and win the 100 meter dash as this photograph shows. It was a surprise victory as Dillard was known as a hurdler and not expected to be a factor in the 100 meter dash. Ironically Dillard did not even qualify in the 100 meter hurdles. After this unexpected victory Dillard and his teammates went on to win gold in the 4 X 100 meter relay.

After winning the gold medal for the men's 110 meter hurdles, American Bill Porter pats his silver medal-winning teammate Clyde Scott on the head in congratulations. Porter and Scott were then joined by Craig Dixon, who finished up the United States sweep in the race by winning the bronze medal.

The three decathlon winners pose together after their race. American Bob Mathias, center of picture, was only 17 years old when he won the decathlon gold medal in 1948. Mathias continued to excel in athletics and went on to win the decathlon gold medal again in 1952. Quite the sportsman, Mathias also played in the Rose Bowl that same year.

Summer Fun

By the water

Michigan—Water Wonderla

Plan Your
FLORIDA
Vacation EARLY !

FLORIDA
THE SUNSHINE STATE

Send for This Beautiful Booklet Today !
IT'S FREE !

Many states used advertising brochures to tout the spectacular places to see and exciting activities tourists could enjoy during a visit to their state. Florida called vacationers to its beaches, while Michigan played up the adventures tourists could have around its many lakes.

MIAMI BEACH SOUVENIR SHOP

HENRY BOLTINOFF

"You can always spot visitors from up North ... they're so dark!"

Beachgoers could amuse themselves by collecting shells, basking on the warm sands or braving the crashing waves of a rolling ocean.

JOHN FALTER

SEA BREEZE

ICE

ZG65

In fine weather, a summer day at the lake offered many activities, with water-skiing a favorite among them. The athletic activity appealed to both men and women, and often turned into elaborate competitions between teams and single skiers.

PRINTED WITH PERMISSION FROM AGFA ANSCO

"I let Aldous have a few liberties like that—it stopped his crabbing about the 60 dollars a day we're paying for this."

"We got your card saying 'wish you were here'!"

OCEAN CITY REELS & MONTAGUE RODS

Fishing was a popular pastime on the lake. As this trout fisherman shows, fishing has not changed much since 1948. From the flies hooked on the hat to the cork-handled rod and the wicker creel basket, some fishermen's tools have stood the test of time.

Sporting Nation

Bowling alleys became popular in suburbs and small towns, allowing for league play and making great places to gather during the long winter months.

JOHN FALTER

The return of economic success in the business world made golf courses a popular place to discuss deals and partnerships. In addition, a free round of golf to a would-be client could help develop business relationships.

The Metro Daily News

FINAL EDITION

JUNE 12, 1948

CITATION WINS TRIPLE CROWN

Jockey Eddie Arcaro rides the crowned Horse of the Year to another victory.

kickoff!

As life returned to normal, people showed enthusiastic support for local college and high school football teams. For many, it was the event of the week in the local community.

© 1948 SEPS

Many young men joined the football team not only for the camaraderie, but also to impress female fans.

© 1948 SEPS

Baseball

Ruth bows out with final appearance

The summer of 1948 saw the legendary Babe Ruth bow out of the games of baseball and life.

During a Yankee Stadium anniversary event on June 13, 1948, Ruth stepped to the microphone to thank a lifetime of friends for their support.

On Aug. 16, at 8:01 p.m, Ruth took his final breath. For two days he laid in state at Yankee Stadium, "the house that Ruth built." Funeral services were held at St. Patrick's Cathedral.

Other baseball players honored that year include Lou Boudreau, who was the American League Most Valuable Player and Stan Musial, who captured National league honors.

Here Babe Ruth donates the manuscript of his autobiography to the captain of the Yale baseball team, future president George H. W. Bush.

© 1948 SEPS

Ht. middle ca

"Well, I'll be! … They do look different from back here!"

© I·L·P

orman Rockwell

CHEVROLET

BUICK'S
the one and only
WITH ALL THESE FEATURES

Cars of 1948

Classics in the making

By the standards of many classic car collectors, 1948 was a vintage year. With the war now a few years in the past, automobile designs now focused on style instead of function.

Luxury items started to appear, such as power brakes and power clutches. Convertibles became more popular, with their unique design. With the slow advent of television and the visual marketing world, diversified looks became more and more important in driving sales.

A fine car made even finer

PONTIAC

Cadillac

FUTURAMIC

Dodge

'Jeep' Station Wagon

Tucker '48

This time it's *Hudson*

Cars We Once Knew

DeSoto

REPRINTED WITH PERMISSION FROM CHRYSLER GROUP, LLC

The rise and fall of popular 1948 vehicles

Following the lull of World War II, many manufacturers were attempting to add new features to promote a new car on the rise. Car manufacturer Preston Tucker's 1948 racecar, the "Torpedo," was equipped with new innovations, notably a middle light that turned with the steering wheel.

However, Tucker was soon in trouble for allegedly pre-selling accessories, a practice that was considered illegal and fraudulent at the time. By the end of the year, the plant was considered bankrupt and up for closure.

Other companies that produced cars that were popular in 1948, such as Packard, DeSoto, Studebaker and Nash, faded off the scene in the following decades or merged with other companies after becoming overwhelmed by attempts to jump ahead of the competition.

While these companies are no longer producing cars, many car enthusiasts have restored older models, thus allowing the companies to "live on" for future generations.

Studebaker

REPRINTED WITH PERMISSION FROM THE STUDEBAKER NATIONAL MUSEUM

REPRINTED WITH PERMISSION FROM CHRYSLER GROUP, LLC

Nash

Everyday Life

At the market

Neighborhood markets were often a gathering place where neighbors caught up with the latest news around town while stocking up on their grocery, household, and in some cases, medicinal needs.

Some markets had checkerboards or game tables for those who would like to linger and pass some time. Visiting the market was often a time of treats for the kids and a chance for storeowners to catch up on the latest family tidbits.

Familiarity was the key word; storeowners and cashiers were familiar with most family needs. Forgetful husbands or children could usually be reminded of the reason for their visits to the market by clerks who knew their customers well enough to guess at the forgotten items.

A trip to the local drug store was often a weekly family trip. Children would even bring in their dolls for special care and bandaging from the pharmacist.

Grocery stores in 1948 were often the center of neighborhood life. Groceries were often purchased on consignment. Of course, the grocer was also a source of local news and a good listener.

The Metro Daily News

FINAL EDITION

JULY 31, 1948

TRUMAN DEDICATES IDLEWILD AIRPORT

New York's international airport is later known as John F. Kennedy Airport.

What Made Us Laugh

"Have some butter? *NINETY-TWO CENTS A POUND!!*"

"Darling, will you marry me if I get a raise at the shoe store?"

"Takes a lot of money these days to live in poverty."

"My husband explained inflation to me, Mr. Schmitz, so I'm not angry at you any more."

"It can't be the quality! We make the finest buggy whips in the world!"

"To insure ourselves against any loss, Mr. Hurst, we require the names of two people who will put up the money for us to loan you."

Everyday Life
Looking Good

EARLY AMERICAN
Old Spice

AFTER SHAVING LOTION

Old Spice was, and still is, a popular brand for men's grooming supplies. Aftershave, shaving mugs and brushes, and talcum powder were well-liked gifts as well as necessary items.

with <u>hair</u> like this, you'll hear: "hello, handsome"

EVERY DAY THOUSANDS OF MEN are giving up other shaving methods for

Sunbeam
SHAVEMASTER
REG. U.S. PAT. OFF.

The **ONLY** shaver with the BIGGER **SINGLE** HEAD with greater CONTINUOUS-SHAVING-SURFACE

With the opportunity to freely take business to the road, portable grooming essentials, such as electric shavers made by companies like Sunbeam, Norelco, and Remington, became commonplace in travel bags.

The popularity of Vitalis Hair Tonic rose dramatically when it was marketed as scalp tonic that would groom a man's hair so well he was irresistible to the ladies of the town. Cleveland Indian baseball great Bob Feller promoted the tonic in popular ads.

Vitalis and the "60-Second Work to stimulate scalp...keep hair hands

VITALIS

Product of Bristol-Myers

"I got a haircut today and do you know what the barber said? He said few men my age have such a fine head of hair."

Even the younger generation caught on to the grooming fad. Here a young man is pampered at the local barbershop.

Humming Bird 51

HUMMINGBIRD 51

Women's Style

Foundations and accessories

Women's styles for 1948 focused on beautiful, wearable clothes in saturated colors and dark neutrals. Many designs were inspired by Victorian-period clothing. Rather than staying with the decades-old standards of using soft-ply yarn or crepe fabrics, designers turned to more crisp fabrics, such as taffeta. Tweeds were also popular for coats, suits and skirts.

However, casual fashions for the average woman were equally prevalent and were worn on a daily basis and for almost any occasion.

© 1948 SEPS

"I undressed and dressed myself 27 times while you were getting dressed once!"

Ladie's handbags tended to be longer and slimmer, mostly in pouch shapes. Many purses were made out of leather, both for style and because they were easier to clean.

"It does more than help capture the new look—let's say it keeps it prisoner."

Shoe cobblers were kept busy caring for the year's most popular shoe, the pump. In the evening, the ankle-strap shoe was appropriate, while suede was often worn in the daytime.

Hats were not considered as essential as during the earlier 1940s, but straw or "roof top" hats, bonnets and brimmed hats with veiling were worn in the summer. A variety of small shapes reigned during fall or winter, including cloche, pillbox, beret, calot, turban and bonnets.

The Metro Daily News

FINAL EDITION

AUGUST 25, 1948

HOUSE UN-AMERICAN ACTIVITIES COMMITTEE TELEVISES

The first televised Congressional hearing includes famous confrontation between Whittaker Chambers and accused Alger Hiss.

Women's Style
Glamour

With the hopes that came with a growing economy, many women were able to focus on clothing, accessories and beauty supplies which had been harder to come by and afford during the war. Beauty regimens and shopping showed that glamour was back in style.

Many women preferred to make their own garments. Sewing patterns offered the opportunity to create either casual or business looks.

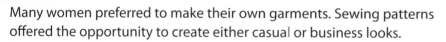

This stylish suit offsets smart accessories, like matching gloves, scarf and hat, that added a glamorous touch to an ensemble.

Women of Mystery
Noir of film and fiction

As with many characters in the film noir and pulp fiction of the era, this woman's eyes betray a slight suspicion and uneasiness as she surveys her situation.

Noir fiction and film often depicted a heavy tension or mistrust between characters even when they were not near or looking at each other.

The look on this woman's face seemingly questions the motives of the man's cuddling approach. But, is it him or her that has something to hide?

© 1948 SEPS

Whether running from something in the night or hiding secret thoughts from a companion, pulp fiction and film noir female characters maintained their often dark sense of mystery.

As Bing Crosby clearly displays in this Stetson advertisement, hats were essential in 1948 for completing a dapper outfit.

Men's Style

The basics

As social life became more active again, there was a large shift to casual evening dress and sportswear after the war.

One addition into men's fashion in the United States was the introduction of Hawaiian and Carissa shirts. First worn on the California and Florida beaches, they featured island-inspired patterns.

The Esquire jacket also emerged in the late 1940s. It was loose-fitting and featured broad shoulders. In addition, double-breasted suit jackets became more popular.

Matching ties and pocket handkerchiefs contrasted with lighter-colored suits were considered to be dashing and eye-catching, grabbing the attention of ladies in the office.

REPRINTED WITH PERMISSION FROM HART, SCHAFFNER & MARX

Colorful patterns
and busy prints
were popular
for ties in the
late 1940s, as is
evidenced by
these paisley
Arrow ties.

Rather than buying a suit straight off the rack, most men at the time had their suits tailored to fit.

A put-together and
well-tailored suit and
tie combination was
expected, even at
casual events.

Look for the
Arrow Trade-mark

ARROW TIES
Paisleys

Men's Style
The accessories

Accessories were a very important part of getting a man ready to face the public. Suspenders, cuff links and properly pressed clothing were all part of the regimen before leaving the house in formal attire.

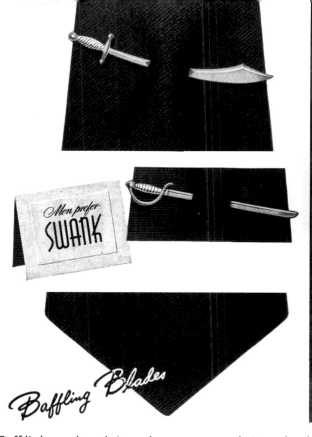

Baffling Blades

Men prefer SWANK

"NOW!
you can't believe your eyes
about cuff links!"

Roblee

SHOES FOR MEN

SUMMER-TONES

Cuff links and necktie tacks were not only in style; they were common gifts for company recognition or from family members. Tie clips were often designed to represent certain community clubs' or organizations' themes

Shoes were often two-tone, with Roblee summer-tones providing styles that allowed feet to breath and be comfortable. Woven patent leather was also popular and easier to polish.

The installation of more comfortable seats enabled passengers to relax and enjoy each other while the world went by outside the train.

America Travels

By train

With a new surge in public interest for travel, and intense competition developing between the railroads, transport lines quickly developed for features that would invite business. Trains began housing upgraded dining and sleeping cars and Pullman even decided to equip some of its cars with air-conditioning.

Train lines began to use new, lightweight passenger cars and shift from steam engines to diesel, with usage of diesel engines more than doubling by the end of 1948.

As the number of passenger trains increased, booming train-business competition demanded that conductors and train employees make a commitment to courtesy and accommodation of customers.

FAMOUS BIRTHDAYS
Robert Plant, August 20 Singer, songwriter and member of band Led Zeppelin

Union Pacific Railroad and Chicago and North Western Railway ran the "City of Portland" passenger train. The line was known for its luxurious baggage, coach and sleeping cars.

America Travels

By train

© 1948 SE

Following the war, many family gatherings depended on the convenience of passenger-train travel. Depots were crowded with those saying "Goodbye" to those leaving, or waiting for relatives who hadn't been seen for long periods of time.

The Western Pacific Railroad was considered to be one of the most scenic on the rails. It offered spectacular views of the San Francisco Bay area, the mountain communities of the Feather River Route, and the deserts of Nevada and Utah.

BETTER TRAINS FOLLOW GENERAL MOTORS LOCOMOTIVES

General Motors Electro-Motive Division, which had been streamlining power cars and experimental locomotives, began to prosper in 1948. The division soon became one of the most popular sources of Electro-Motive Diesels.

The railway system became especially popular for long-distance travel. Families could more easily afford a train ride than a costly airplane trip to visit relatives on vacation or for holidays. Passenger train lines made sure to cater to these traveling families.

Thrill to winter sports

Sight-Seeing! Photography! Best at "Scenery Level"

To fields and forests across the nation

Follow the team

Bus travel gave customers the opportunity to visit, relax and take in stunning scenery. Interestingly, casual dress on such trips was still quite rare, as many traveled in their Sunday best.

TO SNOWLANDS . . . TO SUNLANDS . . .

For winter travel at Lowest Fares—take TRAILWAYS

Trailways ads in 1948 promoted comfort-lined buses with low bargain fares. "There's miles of smiles with Trailways' low fares," stated the advertisements.

America Travels

By bus

After being restricted during the war from purchasing much gasoline, the return to prosperity inspired Americans to once again take to the roads to visit relatives, recreational sites and breathtaking sights.

Many chose to travel by bus instead of taking their own vehicles. Some enjoyed the novelty of bus travel, while others enjoyed the comfort of relaxing and taking in the scenery instead of the tiring task of driving across the country.

Buses also contained many luxuries that weren't standard on automobiles of the time, such as air-conditioning and luxury seats.

Relax... with Greyhound!

Relax Free from traffic worries!

Week-end and rush hour traffic is no bother, with an expert Greyhound driver at the wheel. You arrive rested, refreshed.

Greyhound Bus Company promoted sparing wear and tear on privately owned vehicles while relaxing on long trips by traveling on their buses.

"That settles it !..

with other costs so HIGH and Greyhound fares so LOW...

we'll go Greyhound!

Present costs compared with 1939 prices—latest available records

Bus travel was promoted as being cheaper than any other form of transportation. Greyhound promoted convenience, coverage, comfort and cost effectiveness in long-distance travel.

FAMOUS BIRTHDAYS
Terry Bradshaw, September 2
football player
Bob Lanier, September 10
basketball player
Bryant Gumbel, September 29
broadcaster

Tending to animals was a way of life for those living on the farm, whether it involved cuddling the pets or caring for livestock. Lasting friendships were made with 4-H project animals and family pets.

"Agnes, did you leave the front door open?"

Children on the farm learned responsibilty early, whether it was exercising and feeding the animals, or chipping in with other chores. Everyone had their own set of duties.

"You've been in the mud again"

Life on the farm, including spring planting and fall harvest, was often governed by weather conditions. This meant working long hours when the weather was good and waiting out days when the weather was too bad to allow farm work.

Everyday Life
At the office

ElectronicMemory

In the late 1940s, the electronic memory machine was a new tool for business and enjoyment. The machine initially became famous in the movie industry when Clark Kent, reporter for the *Daily Planet*, could be seen using a similar machine in the 1948 film *Superman*. The more elaborate machines, often referred to as "wire recorders," also contained radio and phonograph capabilities.

Office attire in 1948 included three-piece suits and the latest styles in hats.

The sound of the striking of typewriter keys was still an everyday occurrence at a time when computer keyboards were still many years away.

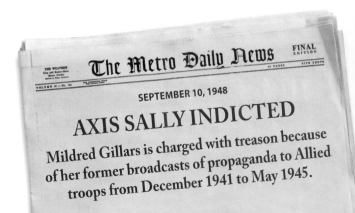

THE WEATHER
City and Suburban
Snow, Colder
Details in Daily Channel

The Metro Daily News

FINAL
EDITION

VOLUME 87 — No. 261

FIVE CENTS

SEPTEMBER 10, 1948

AXIS SALLY INDICTED

Mildred Gillars is charged with treason because of her former broadcasts of propaganda to Allied troops from December 1941 to May 1945.

Women often wore dresses and stylish suits to display a put-together and professional look at the office.

Most companies still had little opportunity for women to achieve senior positions and so maintained a sense of male dominance in a world where professional employment of women was coming into its own.

the Calculator

THAT REMEMBERS WHAT OTHER CALCULATORS FORGET

Burroughs

"Want to hear how you sound backwards, Mr. Denby?"

Everyday Life
School Days

Heading off to college often meant being away from home for long periods of time. College-bound students often transported every conceivable item they felt they might need, including sports equipment, books, study aids, clothing for all seasons, records, food and other miscellaneous items.

Riding to school on a bus was an opportunity to meet new friends and see old ones. At Christmas and special holidays, riders might look forward to such treats as candy, apples and brown paper sacks full of goodies. Older students often enjoyed a bit of mischief in the back seats.

"Y'know, studying can be fun if there are enough people around."

It was a tense moment when students were asked to recite their pieces at the annual Christmas program. Sometimes, the whispers of parents or teachers were needed to help nervous program participants finish their recitations.

There were always those tough days when nothing but the hem of Mother's coat provided comfort, in spite of the attempts of a teacher or classmates to change the mood of the moment.

Everyday Life
Young love

Flowers and formal attire soon gave way to frolic and dancing as the stresses of World War II faded into history.

A young lady out for a ride with her ribbon-wrapped ponytail blowing in the wind didn't take long to attract two young sailors.

"Would you mind kissing her more quietly, sir? You're disturbing the other patrons!"

What Made Us Laugh

"Yes, I am waiting for anyone, thank you."

"Ah, those will be the days."

"I warned you not to go out in the garden with him"

"You're just trying to distract me, aren't you?"

"I feel a little chilly, Lester. Will you run inside and get me Jack Davis?"

"Remember, men—he's probably armed, so it's important that we take him by surprise."

"It just so happens that I like Mexican Chihuahuas and I'm not in any particular hurry."

"Gerald! You're not listening to a word I'm saying!"

U.S. NATIONAL OCEANIC & ATMOSPHERIC ADMINISTRATION

NARA, TRUMAN LIBRARY

On May 30, 1948, Vanport, Ore., received a brutal shock, when a dike restraining the Columbia River collapsed during a flood. The entire city was underwater by the end of the day. Much of the city was destroyed, including one of the largest public housing projects in the country. Traffic came to a standstill and cars were abandoned as the town's residents attempted to flee. Although President Truman voiced his concern over the situation and visited Vanport in June to inspect the flood damage, many thought that the government failed to provide adequate assistance to the town.

The end of October 1948 was an especially scary Halloween for the residents of Donora, Penn. Seemingly straight out of a science fiction movie, a mysterious fog began to cover Donora on October 27th. The smog became a lethal combination of fog and pollution, and covered the town for four days. During this time, hundreds of animals died, thousands of people were sickened and 20 people died. Now the "Killer Smog" of Donora is remembered as one of the worst examples of pollution in America's history.

Weather Extremes

1948 brought several episodes of intense climate conditions. Throughout the year, near disasters and true devastations occurred because of strange and threatening weather. Americans were caught off guard by several floods and numerous tornados. 195 tornados were reported for the year, which numbered 53 more than the usual average for the 25 years before 1948. October brought the infamous "Killer Smog" to Pennsylvania and December brought record snowfalls to New England. New Yorkers had to bundle up and start shoveling after a heavy snowstorm left the city covered in snowdrifts several feet deep.

JOHN FALTER

Building Boom

America develops

The increase in population following World War II created a growing market for new schools, hospitals and housing subdivisions.

While the end of the war brought a close to many industries, several companies adapted their manufacturing to fit the needs of postwar America. Industries like aluminum manufacturing and aircraft production were expanding in the midst of a housing boom and increased air travel.

BETTER ROADS f

President Truman's signing of the Federal Highway Act of 1948 on June 29 created thousands of jobs through highway improvement programs.

With the rising economy, there was more call for shopping-center development, which opened up new building opportunities.

In addition, many veterans who were receiving educational opportunities through the GI Bill were able to contribute to the growing workforce with new skills and knowledge they acquired in college.

BETTER WORLD

© 1948 SEPS

Air conditioners were still quite rare, but some fortunate people introduced them into home life. Most families, however, still cooled their homes with fans during the daytime and with open windows in the evenings.

JOHN FALTER

Years Ahead...

THE YORK ROOM AIR CONDITIO

Modern Home Convenience

Making life easier

The arrival of the postwar boom and its prosperity quickly converted into efforts to make life more convenient, especially around the house. Although primitive by today's standards, many early conveniences started to make their way into the market in 1948.

While central air-conditioning was years away, window air conditioners started to enter the homes of the more well-to-do; as did appliances such as washers, dryers, large ironers and dishwashers.

The arrival of such home-convenience items spurred an industrial revolution that grew into the thriving economy of the late 1940s and 1950s.

Up until the origin of washing machines, most individuals, especially in rural areas and small towns, had designated Monday as "wash day" and had hung their clothes on the line following cleaning. The coming of clothes dryers would eventually alter that routine forever.

"Watch daddy when the toast pops up."

© 1948 SEPS

The emergence of ironers made things much easier for those who had stood on their feet and pressed the family laundry for hours.

Very few families could afford automatic dishwashers in 1948, but for a world in which working women were becoming more common and gender roles were less defined, the new invention proved delightfully useful.

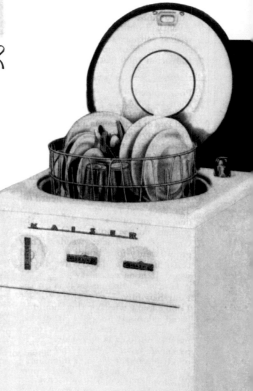

Everyday Life

The changing face of home entertainment

World War II sparked many innovations and technologies that made their way into the American home in the postwar years. As economies recovered, the dream of having a wireless radio, a phonograph or even a television was no longer so unachievable. Manufacturers and advertisers picked up on this trend and portrayed the home-entertainment center as a place for families to gather together and enjoy themselves.

"Here's something you might like. It looks like a radio-phonograph but actually it's a cabinet."

This table-sized record player boasted that it contained a "New Console-type Record Changer." Record players in 1948 also had to accommodate the new 33⅓ size Long Playing record that came out that year.

Although televisions were still quite expensive in the United States in 1948, innovations were being developed to give Americans a quality product at a reasonable price. Hallicrafters even offered a small-sized television that would be more affordable and convenient for some families.

While some companies sought their share of the market with smaller entertainment pieces, other companies, like Admiral, went for top-of-the-line everything-included entertainment centers. Admiral's "Triple Thrill" included a drop-down wireless radio, a fairly large-sized (for the time) television in the center and a pull-out phonograph that would play different sized records.

Many companies also wanted to emphasize the sheer entertainment value of their products. Rather than just being necessary to listen to important news, this console allows the whole family to enjoy themselves while listening to fun music.

Everyday Life
Mischief and Mayhem

"I saw the bear when I was takin' this, but I didn't say nothing cause I was afraid everybody'd move too fast and spoil the effect!"

The old adage "two heads are better than one" often applied quite effectively to sisters conniving behind their mother's back about the most "convenient way" to accomplish their purposes.

Automobiles were always a temptation to the neighborhood gang, even if they required a lot of work.

"Who's running the water down there? How's a guy supposed to get a drink?

Clotheslines often provided a protective cover for young boys seeking to sneak behind Mother's back after ruining good clothes. Unfortunately, an opening between clothes often provided a "catching glance" from Mom.

LIBRARY OF CONGRESS, PRINTS AND PHOTOGRAPHS DIVISION

On the Campaign Trail

Presidential election

1948 brought a shocking presidential election that was, perhaps, the most famous election upset in American history. It was widely believed that Republican Thomas E. Dewey would easily nab the title of president. However, the incumbent president, Harry Truman, defied predictions and was re-elected. President Truman's win came after a long struggle in which he almost lost the nomination during the Democratic Convention in July due to his low standing in the polls.

Although posters welcomed Dewey with confidence of his victory in the upcoming elections, Dewey still seems to have a bit of apprehension showing on his face upon his return from his campaign tour.

NARA, TRUMAN LIBRARY

President Truman often took the opportunity to portray himself as a family man during his travels. Here, Truman smiles with his daughter, Margaret, during a campaign tour in Detroit, Mich.

Democratic presidential candidate Harry Truman captured the hearts of small-town America with a whistle-stop tour during the presidential campaign.

NARA, TRUMAN LIBRARY

The candidates had met before the final days of the election. Here, President Truman shakes then governor of New York Dewey's hand at the dedication of Idlewild Airport, meeting for the first time since they had both been nominated by their parties to run for the presidency.

NARA, TRUMAN LIBRARY

The Deway-Truman presidential race was hotly contested on all fronts, as depicted by this illustration of family members vehemently disagreeing over the candidates.

This little boy proudly waits for his picture to be taken in front of the White House, evoking a famous Napoleonic pose. Inside, President Truman displays his own proud attitude as he settles in for some official government business.

THE SATURDAY EVENING

POST

SEPTEMBER 25, 1948　　15¢

A NEW KELLAND SERIAL

IS OUR NAVY TRAPPED IN CHINA?

By Darrell Berrigan

A Complete Novelette

The President in Office

President Truman and Vice President-elect Alben Barkley wave their hats and grin to the crowds after the election results are revealed.

After his surprising victory in the 1948 elections, President Truman settled back into his role. He continued to reach out to American citizens while trying to reassure them of the state of the nation in the post-World War II period. Truman's Presidency was filled with challenging foreign affairs, which he did his best to deal with in a manner benifitting both the United States and foreign nations. Truman's decision to sign the Marshall Plan was a perfect example of his thoughtful and somewhat protective foreign policy.

NARA, TRUMAN LIBRARY

Truman often brought his wife, Bess Wallace Truman, and daughter, Margaret, on the train for his famous Whistle Stop Tour during the presidential campaign.

Seen here in office prior to his re-election, President Truman shakes hands with Gen. Omar Bradley, who had just been sworn in as Chief of Staff of the U.S. Army. Standing in the background as a witness is Gen. Dwight Eisenhower, hero of World War II.

NARA, TRUMAN LIBRARY

After hearing the results of the election, Truman lifts up to photographing crowds the erroneous *Chicago-Tribune* newspaper that declared "Dewey Defeats Truman" in large block letters. The *Tribune's* premature response became a legendary faux pas in the newspaper business.

ARSHALL

ICE OF THE

STATES

D BY

E CONGRESS

ED STATES

LXXXIV

"Oh, look, Ralph, it's ten o'clock. Let's tune in on the convention."

"I just hope a Republican gets in and tears it right down again!"

Although tensions could be strong between people following the party conventions and presidential race, there were still some citizens that stayed out of politics altogether. These ladies neglect the wonders of the capital city to focus on a young tour guide.

"Are you now, or has any of you ever been a member of the Democratic party?"

"House detective? There's a Democrat in my room!"

Post War Anecdotes

The Navy Cooled Her Heels

A   P O S T   W A R   A N E C D O T E

BEFORE the war it was customary to allow civilians aboard Navy ships during visiting hours on Sunday. The Saratoga, which was anchored in the San Pedro-Long Beach area, attracted a lot of these visitors, and usually they found its decks as steady as their own front porches. Occasionally, however, a freak wind would raise swells behind the breakwater, and if these swells hit the Saratoga broadside, she would roll most heartily. When this happened, the visitors were loaded into running boats and taken quickly ashore.

One stout matron was so resentful at having her visit cut short in this way that the officer of the deck had to have her escorted to the accommodation ladder in order to get her off on the last visitors' boat. This ladder is simply a set of open steps leading down the side of the ship from the deck to a small platform near the water, from which the visitors step into the shoregoing boats. The O. D. carefully cautioned the lady to stay off this platform until he gave the word, but she was too angry to pay attention. Head high, she stepped briskly down to the platform and waited for the boat.

Meanwhile the Saratoga had completed its swing in one direction and was rolling back. The platform started down, hit the water; the O.D. shouted another warning, but by this time the chill harbor water was well above the woman's ankles.

Gasping with surprise and indignation, she glared up at the helpless O.D. "You young whippersnapper!" she roared. "You did that on purpose!"

—COMDR. M. A. PEEL, JR., (SC) USN.

Set a Stick to Catch a Thief

A   P O S T   W A R   A N E C D O T E

NO self-respecting village in India is without its thief catcher—a man who is part detective, part psychologist and part magician. When a wallet was stolen from an Indian soldier under my command, and investigation proved that the culprit must be one of the victim's seven tentmates, I called in Ambika Das, the thief catcher of Kojatoli.

At seven o'clock in the morning he arrived, clean-shaven and smartly dressed, asked the men a few routine questions, then said, "I must now go and meditate. By tomorrow the thief will be discovered." That evening he returned and said to the men, "Here are seven sticks, each seven inches long. Each of you will sleep with one beneath your pillow. By morning, one stick will have grown two inches longer, and I shall know that the head which sleeps on this stick is the head of a thief."

The soldiers went to their tents, visibly awed. But I was less impressed. "You don't really believe all this, do you?" I scoffed.

Ambika Das smiled enigmatically. "Perhaps not, sahib. Nevertheless, you shall see how the thief reveals himself."

At dawn, Ambika Das came and inspected the sticks. Then he pointed to one of the men, who confessed that he was the culprit. To hide his guilt, the thief had cut two inches off his stick.

—EUGENE SAERCHINGER.

The Unexpendables

A   P O S T   W A R   A N E C D O T E

TRAINEES on field maneuvers near a large Signal Corps camp were at a record peak of morale—if you accepted the maxim that soldiers who do the most griping have the highest morale.

Perhaps the commanding colonel was deliberately trying to send morale even higher when he issued a three-word order that was to become famous among Signal Corpsmen.

The outfit was crossing a river under simulated battle conditions. A misplaced explosive charge overturned one of the boats, and a squad of trainees and a crate of messenger pigeons were tossed into midstream. As the noise of "battle" was stilled momentarily, hundreds of men in the other boats heard the colonel's booming command:

"Save the pigeons!"

—FORREST B. JENSTAD.

The Many Arms of Morpheus

AFTER a couple of years in the New Guinea jungles, I developed a fever which the medics promptly diagnosed as F.U.O.—fever of undetermined origin. I was packed off to a near-by base hospital, where for three days I burned and stewed without decisive help from the medical staff.

Then, one night, long after midnight, I was roused from a deep sleep by a determined ward boy. "Wake up!" he shouted, prodding me vigorously. "It's time to take your medicine!"

I eyed him sulkily from beneath my mosquito netting. "It must be pretty damn important medicine," I grumbled, "to get me up at this hour of the night. What is it?"

He examined the dosage for a moment. Then he barked, "They're sleeping tablets. Come on now, Mac. Sit up and take your sleeping tablets!"

—GORDON W. COWAN.

Landlubber Makes Good

ONE of the men in our group of aviation cadets could not accustom himself to the use of naval terminology for living quarters ashore. He could not train himself to refer to the floor as the "deck," or the window as the "port," nor could he remember that the kitchen was the "galley" and that downstairs was "below." He also conceived a hearty dislike for officers who tried to enforce this terminology on him.

One day while serving as cadet officer of the day, under an ensign who had been particularly sharp about naval vocabulary, a terrific thunderstorm blew in over the base. The ensign hastily put his work in order, so that he could hurry home to his bride, who was extremely afraid of electrical storms, and soon he dashed away in a flurry of orders to the cadet to "secure the ports" and "stand by."

A few seconds after he had departed, the cadet noticed that the ensign had forgotten the keys to his car. Scooping them up, he hurried after the officer, overtaking him just as he reached his car.

"Well, what is it, mister?" the ensign snapped, as large drops of rain began to fall. "Can't you see I'm in a hurry?"

"Sir," the cadet said, holding out the keys, "I believe you've forgotten the oarlocks to your rowboat."

—J. B. GARDNER.

But Every Word Counted

COMPARED to a major I knew in Australia during the war, the Sphinx was a chatterbox. This major never used two words where one would suffice; usually he said nothing in a very quiet way. So, when a sergeant from our company was sent to him to be disciplined for "conduct unbecoming to a noncommissioned officer," we waited eagerly to learn what transpired. We felt sure that in this case the major would have to break down and voice a few extra words.

"Well, what did he say?" we asked the sergeant as soon as he came from the major's office.

"He wasn't very talkative," the sergeant sighed. "He just said, 'Come in, sergeant. At ease. Attention, private. Dismissed!'"

—VIVIENNE KERR.

America's Fascination With the West

Following the end of World War II, America's fascination with Western America and its culture returned. The spirit of rodeos and western shows earlier made famous by Buffalo Bill and Will Rogers was alive again. Westerns dominated the movie theaters as well as the bookstores. Children pretended to be cowboys as they played with their western-inspired toys. The styles of the cowboy and rancher even influenced popular clothing.

Even President Truman was not immune to the call of the West. Here, he tries on Texas cowboy boots after receiving them as a gift while Rep. Ed Gossett shows off his own pair of boots.

Swing your Partner!

John Wayne became an icon of the strong, silent cowboy in his many roles in movies. In 1948 alone, Wayne starred in three westerns. His popularity was a reflection of America's interest in the West.

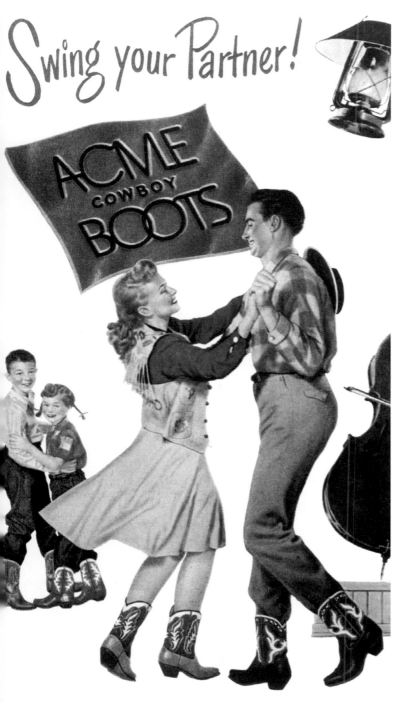

ONE Pendleton CALLS FOR ANOTHER

The boom in western movies carried over to styles, especially in western boots that were often worn for square dancing and other party events.

Plaid and flannel shirts worn with khaki pants became a popular casual style. The look was often advertised as proper attire for hiking, exploring and camping, despite the neatness of the put-together outfits.

Exploring the West

Keep Cool
all the way to
Colorado

© 1948 SEPS

Visit
NEW MEXICO
THE LAND OF ENCHANTMENT

Western states would lure visitors to their land using visually enticing images like these of Colorado and Bryce Canyon. Visitors that made the long journey could enjoy vast lakes, rugged scenery and activities like horseback riding.

Some states promised that the long car ride would be worth the trip to the West in order to learn about Native American cultures. Cross-cultural interplay brought an informed awareness to Americans who might not have had any idea of what life was like for Native American groups in the 1940s.

These cowboys turn back to traditional forms of transport and rely on the strength of their horses to pull a broken-down car through a stream.

What Made Us Laugh

"In tonight's mystery play here are the characters in order of disappearance"

"Of course in the actual show, he really fires the pistol."

"For the last time, Hartnig—stop showing me your home movies!"

"Hereafter, when I send you to a tourist camp to look for food—I expect you to come back with food."

"Yes, he's terribly lazy—just does enough work to barely get by."

"I suppose this means we'll be late again!"

The accessibility of cheaper, more elaborate Christmas lights encouraged entire Christmas tree lighting parties for churches and communities. The camaraderie of such an event often brought a greater holiday closeness to the community.

Everyday Life

Christmas and Community

A combination of old-fashioned tradition and the emergence of modern Christmas activities and decorations, such as electric lights, united communities in Christmas festivities, such as tree lightings and carol singing.

Frequently, the entire community would come together to honor Christmas traditions through manger scenes and music festivities.

The appearance of Santa Claus with treats would often follow the colorful events, bringing together the community with a family spirit that continued throughout the entire season.

© 1948 SEPS

COURTESY OF THE HALLMARK ARCHIVES. HALLMARK CARDS, INC.

Many people followed the tradition of sending Christmas cards, which became more common as the cards themselves became more prevalent and affordable. Some companies, like Hallmark, used paintings from popular artists on their cards, like these reproductions of Norman Rockwell's art, at right.

A visit from Santa was one of the highlights of the year. In the case of small towns, children were amazed that Santa knew their names and certain tidbits about their backgrounds.

MORE TOYS!

MORE ACTION!

MORE COLOR!

Everyday Life

Kids and their toys

The popular word game "Scrabble" made its debut into American homes in 1948 and soon became a souce of stimulation and fun on cold winter nights or at family gatherings.

Many of the favorite toys of the time were interactive. Family members would gather around the card table to construct cabins made of Lincoln Logs. Building bricks were also popular, as was the game Cootie and model airplanes were becoming more desired as toys. Other item making their way under Christmas trees included Jack-in-the-box and electric trains.

Quite often the toys of the time caught the fascination o parents and children alike, who shared mutual enjoyment after dishes were put away and homework was completed in the evenings.

Sleds were popular Christma gift of the tim Young and ol would gather by snowy hillside close to a froze pond to enjc winter activitie parents would ofte bring hot chocola and cookies to kee their children warr

The Metro Daily News

FINAL EDITION

THE WEATHER
City and Snow—Rain.
Snow, Colder
March is Dally Almanac

VOLUME 97 — No. 161

10 PAGES   FIVE CENTS

DECEMBER 10, 1948

UNITED NATIONS GENERAL ASSEMBLY ADOPTS THE UNIVERSAL DECLARATION OF HUMAN RIGHTS

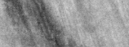

Norman Rockwell

Christmas reunions brought tears of joy as large families welcomed visiting relatives. In this cover, Norman Rockwell included as models his own friends, such as Mead Schaeffer, Grandma Moses, and neighbors Mrs. March and Mary Jarmen, as well as relatives, such as sons Peter, Tom and Jarvis, his wife and himself.

Everyday Life

Christmas and Family

The smells of Christmas filled the air, representing memory-making gifts of family experiences that would be cherished for a lifetime. The scent of hot cider, eggnog and recently baked Christmas cookies blended with the pine scent of a freshly cut Christmas tree.

Families attended the Christmas Eve program at church and then went to bed early to give Santa the opportunity to make his visit to their homes.

Such Christmas poetry as "The Night Before Christmas" was recited by grandparents while dads often read the Biblical Christmas story before prayer at the family Christmas dinner.

Excited children paced all morning, waiting for the arrival of Christmas guests. While they enjoyed their visiting relatives, they also anticipated the armloads of gifts that they would bring with them.

Placing coffee and homemade cookies as a treat for Santa was a custom in many homes. In the morning, children were often delighted to find that he had enjoyed the Christmas snack.

More *The Saturday Evening Post Covers*

The Saturday Evening Post covers were works of art, many illustrated by famous artists of the time, including Norman Rockwell. Most of the 1948 covers have been incorporated within the previous pages of this book; the few that were not are presented on the following pages for your enjoyment.

MORE FAMOUS BIRTHDAYS

January 5
Thom Mooney, Rocker

January 8
Paul King, Rocker

January 10
Donald Fagen, American rock keyboardist

January 12
Anthony Andrews, English actor

January 14
Carl Weathers, African-American football player and actor

January 16
John Carpenter, American film director and composer

January 23
Anita Pointer, Singer

January 29
Marc Singer, Actor

February 1
Debbie Austin, LPGA golfer

February 5
Barbara Hershey, Actress
Christopher Guest, Actor
David Denny, Rock guitarist

February 8
Dan Seals, vocalist

February 14
Teller, Magician and comedian
Pat O'Brien, Reporter

February 15
Art Spiegelman, American writer and cartoonist

February 28
Mercedes Ruehl, American actress

March 4
James Ellroy, American writer

March 8
Little Peggy March, Vocalist

March 13
Robert S. Woods, American actor

March 17
William Gibson, Sci-Fi writer

March 22
Wolf Blitzer, American television journalist

March 25
Bonnie Bedelia, American actress

March 28
Dianne Wiest, American actress

March 29
Bud Cort, American actor

March 31
Rhea Perlman, American actress

April 1
Jimmy Cliff, Jamaican singer and actor

April 4
Pick Withers, Rocker

April 22
Carol Drinkwater, Actress

April 28
Terry Pratchett, English author

May 9
Calvin Murphy, American basketball player

May 15
Brian Eno, Singer and songwriter

May 18
Joe Bonsall, Country singer

May 19
Grace Jones, Jamaican singer and actress

May 21
Leo Sayer, English rock musician

June 18
Nick Drake, Singer and songwriter

June 19
Phylicia Rashad, African-American actress

June 21
Ian McEwan, Author

June 22
Todd Rundgren, American rock singer and record producer

June 23
Clarence Thomas, Supreme Court Justice

July 8
Raffi, Egyptian-born children's entertainer

July 12
Jay Thomas, Actor

July 14
Tommy Mottola, Music manager

July 21
Cat Stevens (Yusuf Islam), English musician

July 28
Sally Struthers, American actress
Gerald Casale, American musician and
    director

July 30
Jean Reno, Actor

August 10
Patti Austin, Soul singer

August 11
Don Boyd, Director

August 19
Tipper Gore, wife of former Vice President
    Al Gore

August 23
Daniel "Rudy" Ruettiger, University of
    Notre Dame football legend

August 29
Charles David Walker, Astronaut

August 30
Lewis Black, American comedian

September 2
Nate Archibald, Basketball player

September 10
Charlie Waters, American football player

September 13
Nell Carter, American singer and actress

September 16
Rosemary Casals, Tennis star

September 17
John Ritter, American actor

September 18
Ken Brett, American baseball player

September 19
Jeremy Irons, English actor

September 22
Jim Byrnes, American actor and musician

September 24
Phil Hartman, Canadian comedian
    (Saturday Night Live)

September 26
Olivia Newton-John, Australian singer and
    actress

October 2
Donna Karan, Fashion designer
Avery Brooks, Actor

October 6
Gerry Adams, Northern Irish politician

October 8
Johnny Ramone, Guitarist

October 11
Daryl Hall, Singer and songwriter

October 14
Harry Anderson, American actor

October 17
Margot Kidder, American actress

October 21
Tom Everett, American actor

October 23
Brian Ross, American journalist

October 29
Kate Jackson, American actress

November 3
Lulu, Scottish singer and actress

November 6
Glenn Frey, Rock musician and vocalist

November 11
Mutt Lange, Zambian-born record
    producer

November 14
Charles Philip Arthur George, Prince
    Charles

November 20
Barbara Hendricks, American-born
    soprano

November 24
Steve Yeager, Baseball player

December 2
T. Coraghessan Boyle, American author

December 6
Keke Rosberg, Finnish Formula One
    champion
JoBeth Williams, American actress

December 12
Tom Wilkinson, English actor

December 12
Ray Jackson, Rocker

December 13
Ted Nugent, Guitarist

December 25
Barbara Mandrell, Singer and television
    personality

December 27
Gérard Depardieu, French actor

December 31
Donna Summer, American singer

Facts and Figures of 1948

President of the U.S.
Harry S. Truman

Vice President of the U.S.
Vacant (Truman, who had been vice president before Franklin Delano Roosevelt's death, never appointed a V.P. when he took over as president)

Population of the U. S.
146,631,000

Births
3,637,000

High School Graduates
Males: 563,000
Females: 627,000

Average Salary for full-time employee:
$2,900.00

Minimum Wage (per hour): $0.40

Average cost for:

Bread (lb.)	$0.14
Bacon (lb.)	$0.77
Butter (lb)	$0.87
Eggs (Doz.)	$0.72
Milk (gal.)	$0.44
Potatoes (10 lbs.)	$0.57
Coffee (lb.)	$0.51
Sugar (5 lbs.)	$0.47
Gasoline (gal.)	$0.26
Movie Ticket	$0.36
Postage Stamp	$0.03
Car	$1,250.00
Single-family home	$7,700.00

© 1948 SEPS

Notable Inventions and Firsts

April 30: The Land Rover is introduced at the Amsterdam Motor Show

June: *The Ed Sullivan Show* begins airing on CBS under the name *Toast of the Town*

June: Bell Telephone Laboratories announces invention of the transistor

June 8: The Porsche 356 is road-certified in Austria

Oct. 19: High Octane gasoline patent issued to Donald Campbell, Homer Martin, Charles Tyson and Eger Murphree, four inventors working for Exxon.

Oct. 23: James Leroy Brown becomes first African-American to receive his wings under the Naval Aviation Cadet Program

Sports Winners

NFL: Philadelphia Eagles defeat Chicago Cardinals
NBA: Baltimore Bullets defeat Philadelphia Warriors
World Series: Cleveland Indians defeat Boston Braves
Stanley Cup: Toronto Maple Leafs defeat Detroit
    Red Wings
The Masters: Claude Harmon wins
PGA Championship: Ben Hogan wins

Dr. Alfred Kinsey causes a stir with the Kinsey Scale, released in his book *Sexual Behavior in the Human Male*

George de Mestral, a Swiss engineer, develops Velcro after studying the fastening effects of burrs on clothing

Edward Lowe introduces and markets Kitty Litter, the first litter using clay granules

REPRINTED WITH PERMISSION FROM REVERE COPPER PRODUCTS, INC.

© 1948 SEPS

Live It Again 1948

PROJECT EDITOR	Richard Stenhouse
ASSISTANT EDITOR	Erika Mann
ART DIRECTOR	Brad Snow
COPYWRITER	Jim Langham
MANAGING EDITOR	Barb Sprunger
GRAPHIC ARTS SUPERVISOR PRODUCTION ARTIST	Erin Augsburger
COPY EDITOR	Amanda Scheerer
PHOTOGRAPHY SUPERVISOR	Tammy Christian
NOSTALGIA EDITOR	Ken Tate
COPY SUPERVISOR	Michelle Beck
EDITORIAL DIRECTOR	Jeanne Stauffer
PUBLISHING SERVICES DIRECTOR	Brenda Gallmeyer

Printed in China
First Printing: 2010
Library of Congress Number: 2009904215
ISBN: 978-1-59635-274-2

Customer Service
LiveItAgain.com
(800) 829-5865

1 2 3 4 5 6 7 8 9